A Story of Saint Lawrence

By
Brother Lawrence Emge, C.S.C.

Pictures by
Carolyn Lee Jagodits

Neumann Press
Gastonia, North Carolina

Nihil Obstat:
Father Edward M. Wetzel, C.S.C.
Censor Deputatus

Cum Permissu:
Brother Donatus Schmitz, C.S.C
Provincial

Imprimatur:
†Most Rev. Leo A. Pursley, D.D.
Bishop of Fort Wayne-South Bend

First Printing 1961

A Story of St. Lawrence

ISBN: 978-1-5051-2097-4

Printed and bound in the United States of America.

Neumann Press
Gastonia, North Carolina
www.TANBooks.com
2021

DEDICATION

to

my mother and father,

Brother Lawrence Miller, C.S.C.

and

Sister Mary Lawrence, O.S.B.

Ferdinand, Indiana

A STORY OF SAINT LAWRENCE

It is really a pity that so little is known about Saint Lawrence. He is one of the most famous martyrs of the early Christian Church, and is among the most honored. We are not told where and when he was born, nor who his parents were. We do know that, though he was very young, he was one of the seven deacons of the Church in Rome. From this we know that Lawrence must have been well educated and, most of all, that he was very holy. Only a person with such good qualities would have been given a high position of great trust like that.

Christians living in the days of Lawrence could not practice their faith openly. Evil men, prompted by the devil, did their best to destroy the Church. Christians lived as much as possible like everyone else so as not to attract attention. As often as they could, though, they stole away to one of the catacombs. In these underground caverns they gathered for the Holy Sacrifice of the Mass, the Sacraments, prayers, and mutual encouragement.

In the year 257, things began to get worse. In most respects, April 1 of that year was a typical spring day in Rome. Even in the early morning hours the narrow streets were filled with people, most of them merchants and housewives getting ready for another day's bargaining.

One person, distinct from the rest, was a well-

dressed man named Vincent. He looked worried about something as he hurried down the street. Presently, he turned into the courtyard of a well-to-do home. Running up the wide outside stairway to the second floor, he entered a room where his friend, several years younger than himself, was studying. He said excitedly:

"Lawrence, I came through the marketplace

on my way over here. Have you heard about the decree that Valerian just published?"

"Well, no, I . . ."

"It says that everyone, without exception, has to worship the pagan gods, and you know who he means when he says that!"

"Yes, Christians, of course. It looks like real trouble is starting for us again, Vincent."

"Yes, things have been fairly peaceful these past three years: the Roman Emperors can't seem to forget about us," sighed Vincent.

"But Valerian has been somewhat favorable to us. What could have provoked him? We haven't done anything to cause it," said Lawrence.

"Well, you know how much his advisor, Macrian, has been influencing him lately. The emperor is superstitious anyway, but old 'Max' has been getting him interested in Persian black magic.

I heard just the other day that Max has been trying to convince him that since Christians are enemies of black magic and the pagan gods, they will bring him, and the whole empire, bad luck. He's told Valerian that the gods will turn their anger on him because he permits some of his subjects to despise them. This decree proves that Max did a good job in convincing him."

"Is that all it says?" Lawrence asked.

"No, it also forbids us to gather in the catacombs any more. If we don't obey, we're in danger of exile or even death, and no doubt he means business."

"Yes, I guess so," Lawrence said with a sigh. "We will just have to pray for strength to endure whatever comes. I'm sure any Christian would rather die than insult Almighty God by worshipping some pagan hunk of marble. Old Diana,

Mars, Apollo and the rest of them won't get any incense from us."

They talked for a while longer and then Vincent departed. Being a deacon of the Church, he had duties to perform.

Even though the Christians ignored the decree of the Roman Emperor, nothing at all happened. The rest of April, May, June and July slipped away. On August 2, as the hot sun sank to the horizon, Lawrence made his way to one of the catacombs. When he reached the large underground assembly room, he was delighted to see Pope Stephen himself there, preparing to celebrate the Holy Sacrifice. Things went as usual until shortly after the Consecration. A shock of fear went through Lawrence when he heard Roman soldiers coming down the passageway. They stood in the back of the room, but Pope Stephen went on with the Mass as if nothing

were wrong. After finishing, he walked slowly to his papal throne nearby, sat down, and bowed his head in prayer.

The silence was broken when the soldiers stomped up the length of the room to where he sat.

"Are you Stephen," one of them said roughly, "the leader of these stubborn Christians?"

"Yes," he said without moving.

"The emperor says he's given you time enough to obey his command," the soldier shouted. "Since you keep on opposing him, you'll have to learn the hard way."

Speaking these words, he raised his sword and brought it down with all his might on the neck of the bowed man. Marching out of the room, the soldier snarled to the congregation:

"And if you don't change your ways, that will happen to all of you!"

All the faithful were shocked and deeply grieved by the death of Pope Stephen. Life had to go on, though, so before very long, minds turned to the question of who would become the new Supreme Pontiff. The choice was an easy one because, living in Rome at that time was a holy old priest named Sixtus. For many years he had been an example to all the Christians by his courage in the face of danger, his humility, and his great concern for those in his care. They were very pleased when he became Shepherd of the whole Church. Lawrence was especially happy because Sixtus was his teacher, whom he greatly admired. The gentle priest had taught him not only how to use his intellect well, but how to love and serve God to the best of his ability. As the years of training went on, a solid friendship grew up between the two.

One day in September of 257, a short time after Sixtus was elected, he and Lawrence were talking. After a while the Holy Father said:

"Lawrence, I made a decision yesterday that I know will make you very happy."

"Oh?" Lawrence said inquisitively.

"You told me many years ago that you wanted to become a deacon of the Church some day, and I

know you still have that desire. Since I don't think it's necessary to wait any longer, I'm going to make you one a week from today. Not only that, you are going to be my chief helper: you'll be Archdeacon of Rome."

Lawrence looked at him somewhat bewildered.

"Now, never mind how young you are; I'm well aware of that," Sixtus said with a smile. "I've known you almost all of your life and I'm sure you are capable. Besides that, you will have to be going all over the city on missions, and Valerian's men will never suspect who you are."

Lawrence was indeed happy. As a deacon he could serve God and his fellow man better. He didn't consider himself worthy of the honor bestowed upon him, but he trusted in his old friend's wisdom. As archdeacon, he was to guard the treasures of the Church and to go about giving alms to the poor people of Rome. He also would assist the pope in saying Mass by taking care of the altar, especially the chalice; reading the Holy Gospel; by bringing the gifts of bread and wine to the altar at the Offertory and by distributing the Precious Blood to the faithful at Communion.

After Lawrence was ordained a deacon, he performed his duties most zealously. One day, after about a month had gone by, we find him visiting a needy home. He said to the father:

"Hello, Prosper, how is everything going with you and the family?"

"Oh, we are all very well — but our cupboard is still rather bare," he added jokingly.

"Ah, yes. So the old senator still doesn't pay you enough to live on, even though you keep his lawns and garden so beautiful," Lawrence said.

"Well, even if we don't have much money, it really doesn't matter. We still have a lot to be thankful for."

"I'm glad you think that way, Prosper: that's the only way to look at it." Turning to the lady of the house, Lawrence asked, "And how are the boys coming with their catechism, Frances?"

"All three of them are doing fine. Since the

emperor had to go away and fight against the Persians, I can teach them more often. Before that, I had to be afraid someone would overhear us and report that we are Christians."

"Yes, we have to be very thankful to God that Valerian went away. Otherwise, it would have been very bad for us."

As they chatted on, Lawrence left a few Roman

coins on the shelf for them to find after his departure.

And so, with the persecutor many miles away, the Christians in the city could practice their faith in peace. This happy state of affairs lasted only about a year. Like a sudden summer rain, trouble began again.

It was August 6, 258. Before the sun had climbed very far into the sky, Lawrence and his friend, Vincent, set out on foot along the Appian Way. The two deacons had a call to pay on a family living some distance outside of Rome. As they walked along the pleasant green countryside, they didn't know what was happening back in the city. A messenger came out of the senate-house and read an announcement to the people standing about in the square before him.

"Citizens of Rome," he shouted, "the noble

Valerian sends a decree to the senators which is to be obeyed immediately. All bishops, priests and deacons of the Christian sect are to be executed. Any senator or person of rank who professes this Faith is to lose his rank and property; and if he refuses to offer incense to the gods, he is to die. Anyone else who refuses to do this is to be sent in chains to work on the emperor's farms."

When Pope Sixtus heard the news of this terrible precept, he remained calm but went into action immediately. He sent his messengers all over the city to tell the faithful to gather in a little known catacomb, that of St. Praetextatus. Before long, the hiding place was filled. The pontiff, seeing stunned or frightened looks on the faces, and many women and children crying, addressed all with words of encouragement. While he was still speaking, the Roman soldiers found their way to the meeting place and seized him.

In the meantime, Lawrence and Vincent came back to the city, heard what had happened and hastened to be with the Holy Father. As they neared the entrance to the catacomb, they saw the soldiers leading him away. Lawrence, wanting to die for Christ with his old friend, broke into a run and shouted:

"Father, where are you going without your son? Should a priest go to sacrifice without his deacon? What have I done to displease you that you are not taking me with you?"

Looking at each other, their eyes blurred with tears, Sixtus answered:

"I am not leaving you, my son. They'll do away with me quickly because I'm old and feeble, but you

are young and will have to suffer many things before you triumph. You will follow me in a few days. But for right now, I want you to give all the money in the treasury to the poor so it won't fall into the enemies' hands."

The soldiers then jerked Sixtus away and led him to the prefect of Rome, Macrian, Valerian's advisor. Macrian gave the aged man a last chance to save himself by worshipping the idols.

Since he remained firm, he was led back to the catacomb where the faithful were still gathered, and beheaded on his papal throne. Then the soldiers killed Lawrence's friend, Vincent, and three other deacons who were present. Lawrence was deeply grieved at the sight, but he fearlessly came forward to die with them. Instead, he was taken to the prefect.

"I understand," Macrian said, "that your priests use gold and silver cups when they offer sacrifices. You have tapers set in golden candlesticks to light the hiding places when you meet at night, and your treasury is full. Well, turn all of that over to us; the emperor needs money for the war. The god you follow says you are to render to Caesar the things that are Caesar's. The emperor's picture is on the coins, so they belong to him."

Lawrence thought quickly and answered:

"Yes, the Church is indeed rich: it is even richer than the emperor. I'll show you our treasures, but give me a few days to get them all together."

The prefect was pleased with the cooperation, so he granted the request.

In the days that followed, Lawrence went about the city finding the lame and the blind, the widows, orphans, virgins and all the poor that the Church supported.

"Here," he said, "take these treasures and hide them until later, and use this money well. There's a favor I want of you, though. Be in the city square at 9 o'clock on August 10. I'll do the rest."

At the appointed time, Lawrence took the prefect to see the assembly.

"What are all these horrible people doing here?" Macrian shouted impatiently. "I told you I wanted your treasures."

"These are the treasures of the Church," he answered. "They don't have any money, so they put all their trust in God. Those that are crippled wait for perfect health and happiness in heaven. Those that are blind are waiting to see

God face to face. They are pleasing to God so He hears their prayers and the Church is made rich with His blessings. If you want me to, I'll ask them to pray for you, Valarian, and all of Rome."

The prefect was red with rage and screamed:

"You mock me! You say that these wretches could be of advantage to us? That's an insult to the Roman Empire! I know what your game is. You want to be a hero and die a martyr. Ha! I'll make you a martyr, all right; but it won't be as easy as you expect. You'll die by inches!"

That afternoon when he was led to the place of execution, Lawrence saw what the prefect meant. Macrian had ordered a large gridiron to be made, and nearby was a pile of red hot coals. The prefect waited eagerly for Lawrence to plead with

him for mercy, but his courage didn't waver. In a fury at being disappointed, Macrian ordered Lawrence chained to the gridiron and placed over the coals.

The fire slowly burned his body, but Lawrence didn't groan or cry out in pain. He kept his eyes on the cloudless blue sky as if he could already see his Lord and Master face to face.

"I can feel the love of God burning in my heart more than the flames under me," he said.

After a long time, Macrian's vengeance cooled down and the novelty of the whole affair wore off because it didn't turn out as he had expected. Grumbling something under his breath, he started to leave.

"Why are you going, Max?" Lawrence said playfully. "Is it suppertime? I'm roasted enough on this side, why don't you turn me over and eat now?"

Macrian insulted him and stalked away.

A short time later, Lawrence sighed heavily and said:

"I offer my life willingly because my Lord suffered so much more when he hung on the Cross for love of me."

After praying that the city of Rome would

give up the worship of idols and be converted to the One True God, his soul went to its reward.

A few senators who witnessed Lawrence's great courage were so impressed that they became Christians. They buried his body in the catacomb of St. Cyriaca on the Tiburtine Way. A shrine was later built on the spot and enlarged several times through the years. Today a great basilica stands on the sight called Saint Lawrence Outside the Walls.

His feast is celebrated on the day he died, August 10.

The End